WANDERING ON THE OUTSIDE

Poems By
Karren La Londe Alenier

With Foreword By **Deirdra Baldwin**

SECOND EDITION

THE WORD WORKS, INC. Washington, D.C.

First Edition, 1975
Second Edition, 1978

Printed in U.S.A.

Library of Congress Catalog Card Number: 74-30470

International Standard Book Number: 0-915380-00-5

Table Of Contents

Foreword

The some time I have known Karren Alenier's work began in 70 with a workshop. (We met for the first time in the spring, here at the farm, with Paul Jones, a poet who moved ex Washington to Chicago and Dan Washburn, a psychologist who invented a self-behaviorist gizmo which, upon the resumption of certain negative habits, produced a mild electric shock. Karren at that time could speak French and COBOL. At present she studies Spanish on her own, works with a feminist organization called FEW, and is a Systems Analyst for the Manpower Administration.) I had difficulty reading her poems. I found them both compelling and bewildering. She was certain of them. And they were certain of themselves. Tightly sealed objects. Individual. Impenetrable. They were sculptures.

***I think that now.** (Of Alenier, Jones said upon meeting that she possessed a "latent beauty." The phrase is still apt. She is extremely private. Her application to life is rigorous, relentless. Where there is not that quality of serious intention, there is a marriage of sublimity with giddiness.)*

*Her work presents two aspects of complexity: the "pivotal line" and something I'll call "point of entry." Now, the "pivotal line" has to do with what William Empson called ambiguity number 5 or a "fortunate confusion." It is the line that demonstrates how a poem evolves of its own language spontaneously, and it enables two mutually contradicting states to exist at one time. This "pivotal line" gathers the poem to itself, producing a grammatical tension. What the line effects externally is the distance between the poem and the reader, reminding the reader of the nature of the communication, the medium, if you please. Enigmatically, the line also represents the unconscious (subjective in the extreme) moment of the poem **when a thought drops** the reader deep into the subterranean world of the poet.*

Internally, that is within the network of the poem itself, the "pivotal line" serves grammatically and is included in the linguistic sense of at least two thought units within the poem. As such it is a floater. A liquid line. Further meaning is dislodged by displacement of the line. By its movement away. Its absence.

To illustrate the operation of the "pivotal line," I cite the poem, "From Shock." That line "what falls in the well" refers back to the sense of "a black hole" and forward to "(well) meant realm." Note the effect of displacement. And again in the poem "Invitation," the line which is a single word "view" is the end of one thought and the beginning of another simultaneously.

Back to "point of entry." How do you approach these poems for which there is very little precedent in contemporary poetry? They do not depend particularly on color or vowel pattern or on a worked language. But on a progression of thought which is inseparable from the language of its expression. If you were to look for a root, you might do well to turn to Wallace Stevens, for like that jar in Tennessee, the human incident is placed against a backdrop of time and space...

WANDERING ON THE OUTSIDE addresses itself to the "one dimensional man" of Marcuse and, in his footsteps, Slater's "outsider." With technology a postulate. In "Unspoken," a delicate analogy is made by placing a mother's breast in contrast to the technology of the cathode ray tube. There is "not satisfaction...just a ripple of milk..." And the last line "no mouth" reminds us both how alien is the breast which feeds us and how voiceless we are in its presence.

Delineated within these poems is a grotesque reality in which human concerns are parodies of themselves and are parodied against time and motion. In "Waiting," the two figures keep readjusting their position and focus with no indication that there will ever be a solution to their waiting. In "Held up," evil and illusion are a piece of the same cloth. Either the reader or the figure whose ritualized behavior climaxes in a cry "no cowboy/ (no indian)/ could ever understand" is deluded: held up. Objects of grief are revealed in their tender banality when the voice recalls discarding the tissue which is the sum and remainder of "pitifully late tears" in the poem "Tunnels." Only death in a thrust of irony surprises in the last statement: "she never did/ a sudden thing/ in her life." Disbelief. Both life and death assume the quality of illusion. Time and distance bring change, even death. Ambivalence characterizes the American response. And incidents in the personal life of the poet collide, propelling those experiences into another dimension. The U-turn of the funeral procession is juxtaposed to the question: "If I could turn around/ for a moment, Mom/ would you/ stand there/ at the door..."

In "Lessons," fear and anxiety are introduced with the notion of doing. Of balance. One must not spill over into despair. One must master technology. And live well. Live right. The voice asks, "God, aren't you ludicrous?"

How often in this poetry we are yanked back from any romantic or poetic notion. In the poem "View," the figures slide "rear-side down" leaving graffiti and beer cans. Fact. And the group experience is made more real; the names of its members repeated like a chant or charm against evil. And like a prayer. A tenderness. But at the same time we are told that (between the members of the group) "the darkness filled in."

This is poetry of a new source. Karren Alenier's poetry. It will not excuse the reader from an intense confrontation with the actual. Nor will it submit to prescriptive notions of what poetry should do or be. Nor will it apologize for what it is. Perhaps it is, in that sense, one step beyond confessional.

dbb
Avenel Farm
November 16, 1974

For PEARL S. FRIEDENBERG

In whose memory,
this tree
has long
been
growing.

"Americans have a profound tendency to feel like outsiders--they wonder where the action is and wander about in search of it."

Philip Slater
The Pursuit of Loneliness

A Review of my Proceedings at the Advocate's Country Estate

Dear Sandy,

I know a man who apologizes
for everything he does.

Today, I lay in the grass
and my image is everywhere
in your yard.

I have flattened the grass blades
like a baker making gingerbread dolls.

I have abused the translucent aphids
by repeatedly flicking them from my arms
and squashed the tiniest orange insects
who refused the same treatment.

I have gathered the rush of rustling leaves
as though it were my personal ocean.

I have sought and savored every fragrance
and pulled the air up around me for my comfort.

And WHEREAS I don't really believe that
I should thank you for what I have done,
I am not inclined to apologize.

Ballet in Wooden Clogs

Walking
and wanting
to wait...
Walking
but waiting
for alien
echoes
though comitatus
tapping
produced
by rote...
Stepping...
Stepping...
with intense
latin
pride
but
clicking out
adolescent
cocks.

America,

my brother
who gently
makes me do
who provides
strength
when I am
only weak
who shows me
how straight
a steady leg
will be
died
away from home
so long
ago
I am not sure
I ever knew
his name.

Blue Dance Beginning

Though
the slippers
were barely seen
the dress
stood away
from the waist
as the order
of the ballet
dictates.
Faces
were subdued
in lieu
of the pastel brightness
of blue crinolin dresses.
And despite all of this
the line of the toe
as the extension of the leg
did not
go
unnoticed.

View

At twilight,
we climbed
up and over
big, warm rocks
to watch the sun's
pale stripe of pink
sink behind the rocks
on the other side of Wyoming Valley.
The lights in Wilkes-Barre
grew brighter
in the dim
          dimness
           darker
            dark of evening
while we sank our minds
into the calmness that wells up
from a small town in a green valley.
The darkness filled in
      between me and Howard,
      between Howard and Sandy,
      between Sandy and Ray,
                 Ray and Julie,
                 Julie and Jayne.
Only if sleep had overcome us...

But we are not ignorant people.
We had seen the broken beer bottles
and the graffiti on the rocks
and knew the distance
between falling off to sleep
and falling off the ledge where we sat.
So night forced us to slide
rear side down
down the back of the rocks
back to the town
Wilkes-Barre.

Journey

For Gary

Your father
Russian Jew
sailed to this country
did well
on hard work
hand work
never spoke
of the original home
came here
in the bar mitzvah year
perhaps too young
to care
and you
you work hard
and love
hand work
yet speak
of learning a foreign language
and visiting
a country across the sea
without
the remotest hope
of knowing
where your father
had been

The Dancing Woman

The men in the Silver Dollar Saloon
did not know
why she danced
May be she had to
like the man jumping
foot to foot avoiding
the pistol
            packer's
                        shots
except that
            her eyes
                        became
lanterns in a storm
and the old prospector
in his decades-old pants
tight-belted though baggy
(even down to the
                        rolled up cuffs)
told her
            each time he was there
"I wished I was young for you"
and moved to smooth
the folds in her dress
created by a final kick
but she refused by side-stepping his hand
Yet she let
            bigger men
catch her bare arms and stop

the swishing satin of her skirt
as she passed between the rounds
of drinking men
                    sitting with bottles
                and glasses
            and occasional games
It was the preacher
who came to town on a donkey
who pressed the theory so often
that she was gypsy--
dark eyes and hair
except that her skin
was so fair--
that the town drunk
an amazingly broken scholar
swirled the syllables of Esmeralda
through his thick tongue
                    and unbleached teeth
as an echo of no mutual comprehension
As though she did not hear
anything but the music
she would dance until everyone
went home for the night
or was thrown out on the street

Held up

He held
a snake
over his head
(some brown
body glistened
in a parching
western
sun)
He held a
snake over
his head
(some naked
foot stamped
dust clouds
ankle deep)
He held a snake
over his
head
Then his voice
yelled the cry
no cowboy
(no Indian)
could ever understand
And he put his
empty hands
down

Waiting

They waited
on opposite sides
of the street.
She thought she would
play a violin
and let the passersby
toss coins into the black case.
He leaned against a light post
studying a crumpled wrapper
of Marlboro cigarettes
and then, he put out two fingers
and looked at them
as though
they were not his.
She glanced at her wrist
remembering
the borrowed watch
was given back.
He stooped to tie his shoes
and broke a lace.
She looked at the sky
She looked at her foot moving
off the curb to the street
and then, she looked at him fumbling with his shoes.
He did not move to get up
determined to use the broken pieces;

so she walked down the street,
crossed in the breeze of several cars,
and sat down on the curb.
They were waiting
                                        on opposite sides
                                                                        of the street
when he discovered
                                        she
                                                wasn't
                                                        there.

Spring Trip

Howard thought
the tree was dead
crispy brown hung
from every limb
and it wasn't winter
any longer and I
felt the pinching fear
of guilt imagining
a naked tree in front of
our house.

one two three
en francais
un deux trois
the windshield cracked
in a million pieces
my students thought
we are sorcerers.

It was a miracle
how do you tell a tree
shall we giggle like young girls
and waste all our three minutes?

That was a tree in France
and the phones are so bad in Paris
no one answers at the American Embassy
or they leave the receivers unhooked.

When we stopped rolling
We all wanted to know
the state of
O.K.?
O.K.?
One didn't say
and his seat swelled
with the emptiness
of a past tense explosion
when the silence takes its turn
against the bang.

In my life
I want to speak clearly
I want nothing to impede my voice
and I want to hear what is said for myself.
Last week I cleared away
a lot of broken glass
a lot of road dirt
a lot of my husband's blood
and these are no license for life
just chisels
on so many raw edges
I need to redefine
or else laugh
that the tree
in front of our house
was producing its seed.

Outside the day was very bright

(visit with a Berkley carpenter)

He sat
in a rough hewn rocker;
the room
smelling of wood
was very dim.
The floor spread out
in long boards
broken
by a few
woven mats.
We sat
across from him
on a sofa
that didn't match
the sparseness
and the simplicity
of all the wood.
His friend,
who was our friend,
pointing upward
spoke quietly,
"There is the guest room."
It was a shelf
he built
close to the ceiling
supplied with cushions
and a ladder
running down
along the wall.

We turned back to him.
I asked softly,
"How did you think of that?"
The outline
of a full beard
emphasized
the slight, upward movement
of the corners of his mouth
and he rocked a bit.
We looked at him
his eyes,
his face,
his plaid shirt,
the jeans,
the shoes...
We listened to the quietness a while.
It was Ron
who said,
"We enjoyed the visit"
and went to him
and shook his hand.
All standing
saying good-bye at the door
and then squinting
as we walked
from the house.

Displacement

kids and lambs
over the heat grate
in the floor
brought in
from the Midwestern
night cold
I told you
I never heard
such a strange thing
and you explained
how you had
never seen
a Jew
until you
left home
much less
talked
to one

From Shock

This man
did not
speak
his thoughts
a black hole
that pulled others in
to the loneliness
no one saw or felt
who knew
did he
he did not say
what falls in the well
meant realm
people talk
people ask
people come and then leave
this he did hear and see
but now this man
did not
speak

Tunnels

I threw those tissues
down the chute
tonight...
I imagine
they floated down
as Alice's rabbit
puffed and
disheveled--
they were
my pitifully late
tears
a whole
trash can
full...

My mother
told me through the
telephone--
"We had a great loss
pause...pause...pause
"while you were away
pause...
"Mom is dead."
"Oh," I said
though the bottom
of my throat
kept pushing
to the top...

"I didn't know..."
"Three weeks ago...
We couldn't spoil your trip."

I wrote
lots of postcards...
"Dear Mom,
          We're in Zurich
The Limmat River
     is full
     of swans
The cheese fondue
we had today
wasn't as good
                    as mine
                              Love..."

My father told me
the funeral procession
got lost...
Baltimore has a lot
of new roads
and the director
blew the turn
at a confusing fork
but he brought her
to her mother's grave
and apologized

mortified over
U turns with a
funeral procession.

If I could turn around
for a moment, Mom
would you
stand there
at the door...
I'll kiss your cheek.
Your skin was always
so smooth...

I never had
any doubts that
you would be
home...
I do now
though I haven't been
there
to find out...

When Nana died
I knew she was dead.
I think I could see
her nose
as she lay in the coffin...
I couldn't look...

I wanted to remember her face
when I was young
when we went walking
on Charles Street...

Two of my mothers
Two of my mother's mothers
lay side by side in Baltimore.
That I can say...
But I can't believe
that Mom is dead--
She never did
a sudden thing
in her life.

What should I give besides...

Michael, even
if you touched
my hand and trained
your darker brown eyes
into mine
and filled my ears
with the words according to
the formula,
it would be yesterday
that I knew
the syllables into words
into phrases into sentences
had no gravity
that's how they flow
so beautifully, so free
no attachment--
Were you my lover
I would be free
to admire your capacities
and to leave in the morning
while you slept.

Michael, even
if you touched
my hand
I would see
the words on your lips
and let them be said
until there was no more space in our time
and the only thing, Michael,
that protects your life
is that you'll never stop
to ask for
the explanation.

Yahrzeit: A Birth

Ellen
a year
has past
since Etta mother
of your mother
lay down
your head covered
with tufts of black
silk sheened hair
Marilyn
your mother
cried for you
and Ellen you
can answer

Treasure Maps

Your absence
blows through me
like a Kansas wind
free in the empty
streets of night
everyone is home
and are you
warm and at peace
where you are
or do your thoughts
wander as mine
on the well worn routes
noting all the ruts
waiting only
for repair?

Grandmother,

summer
peaches
you loved
how wonderful
you thought
in ice-cream
my mother
your daughter thought
cream and
peaches
your complexion so white
smooth and
child fresh
and this summer passed
without
you
to appreciate
any.

Wunkirle

(Most Hospitable Woman)

After you receive your guests,
come to me, Spoon Mama
on those supple legs--
muscles flowing like milk
and scoop the agony from my gut.
I have got a lot
but your bowl is large
as your reputation
and though the invited
came for rice
give them each
a portion of pain
and let them then
as I will do
thank you
for your generosity.

Bringing up...the obvious

To the woman
in the white
hat that is
hard
work
lady
in the construction
pit
with construction
boots
and bare
arms...
Do the men?
Do your co-workers
whistle
at you
or with you
or are they
too busy
working
as hard as you do
to bring up
the structure?

Mother, don't send your son to the freezer

**It bothers me
that Walt Disney reclines
in a deep freeze
waiting for the scientist (prince)
to create the cure for his disease
He refused return to the earth
like any common man
he refused; he won't leave
so he'll wait like a figure
in Madame Tussaud's
but hoping to be selected
over the box of ice-cream.**

Visiting

Margaret had a yard
a living room
every tree
a precious stick
of furniture.
She said, "Magnificent,
the blossoms are so fragrant."
We said, "Don't fall down.
The magnolia blooms are
so out of reach."
"Nonsense, they're only delicate.
Never touch the petals
or they'll turn brown."
We said, "Margaret,"
She said, "A bouquet for my friends."

Oranges

For Jack

She knew
how
to peel
oranges.
You were
thirsty
but
not interested
in getting
your fingers
wet.
You smiled
extending
the best you had.
she laughed
like a mother
and asked
can't you do it
yourself?

Invitation

What
did the woman think
or did she
die letting you go
your face
so sad and flat
would have been enough
for a mother to
think twice
did you think more
than once
you were born
with the buds of two
skulls behind your ears
and two bodies facing trunk to trunk
like two neck wrung chickens
dangling in the butcher's window
you would escape her
view
the women in this museum
who pause and pause
and roll "Janus Monster" in a jar
through layers of
fertile thought

Unspoken

On the cathode ray tube
words flow like a ripple of milk
down the side of a glass
at breakfast.
Not satisfaction
like a mother's soft tit
pressed face full
in a suckling child.
...just a ripple of milk
down the side of a glass
with absolutely
no mouth.

Sea Pairs
(an old set)

bubbled
bloomers
floating
neck high
thin blue lips
burping
giggles
after...
two jellyfish
we thought we
were safely
alone
we thought we
were serious
so we laughed
grabbing pants
and forgetting
how hard
treading
can be

Lessons

A
bicycle lesson
in a narrow
alley

wobbling

slowly
along

pushing
right hand
left hand

on the rough
brick
walls.

God,
aren't you
ludicrous?

Isn't walking
the marvelous
feat?
swimming?
flying?

Excuse me,
Michael...
do you
remember
your first
step?
No.
but the alley
      the bicycle
       the brickwalls
              wobbling?
What could
reel
in your
mind
more?

At five
you were
let out
of 3 years
on your back
with your leg
in a brace
and a platform shoe.
You know,
I blew it.

Before they let you out
I had my choice
between a 2 or 3 wheeler...
That same tricycle
you fell off
chipping your front teeth
the same day our baby sister
filled her stomach
with a prescription
of mother's pills.

Isn't living
as delicate
a task
as learning
to bike?

Michael,
I don't remember
when
they let you
wear
normal shoes
but we must have been
about 8 and 9.
Time didn't mean
too much then

and it's too late
to ask you now.
Don't we look for time
to cover those events
which were difficult.

But let's not bury
that day
in the alley between
those red brick walls.
I get the feeling
that I'll need
to talk
about it more
as time passes and we come closer to our deaths.
Unlearning to move
will be
balancing
the bike
in one spot
with feet rigid
on the pedals.
I'll need your advice again.
I mean I might need to
practice that
a long time.

Passing out

His whole life
he knew about
emptiness.
He was an
expert
empty pockets
            stomachs
holes in his shoes.
He spent his time
looking for work
ditch digging
donut making
making holes in his
shoes he understood
he was an expert in
living without
the missing chunks.
Yesterday the state lottery
gave him a million bucks
an exchange for
all his expertise.
His mind fell
black with joy
like his body
he didn't even wonder
what his shoes
could hold.

Closed Sets

My face turned
inside out
from the corners
of my mouth
and you saw
my veins
and my arteries.
I pushed my hands
up to my cheeks
and the universe
reversed.
I drank water for days
and stood in the shower
hour on end
on end.
I kept thinking:
the sculptor made my skin
out of eggshells
and kept reviewing why
I needed lessons on how to
breathe in and out.

We talked about
mind sets
and the disappearance of accidents:
if I step into the street
and a car strikes me

am I liable
for having thought the possibility...
for having constructed the idea...
for creating the scene...
How do I phrase
my breath
my breathing in
my breathing out
and avoid
the syncopation
of hiccups?

When I see you
searching my face
looking for eye entry
my mouth starts to switch
and my whole face follows
showing parts of me
I would rather protect.
What unstated idea
between you and me
causes my discomfort?
This behavior is no accident
even a chameleon would be awed.

Building

Feel
like a stone wall
how
could the Chinese perpetuate
those stone miles
my eyelids close
the curves
like the hillside
holding
its fence
no woman now
undulating river
stone piles
textured and impassible:
I can keep the enemies out
the strength
in the stones
like a faith

Mantra for the Whole

It is
Monday and I am
breathing in
and breathing out
holding then
relaxing
waiting for every
opportunity
to move in my
mind washing
every curve
knowing I am
breathing
Tuesday I am
Wednesday/Thursday
breathing in
Friday out
Saturday mind
Sunday washing
It is
Monday and I am